DATE DUE

LITTLE ROCK NINE

JOHN PERRITANO

red rhino b**OO**ks®

NONFICTION

3D Printing	Medal of Honor
Area 51	Monsters of the Deep
Bioweapons	Monsters on Land
Cannibal Animals	The Science of Movies
Cloning	Seven Wonders of the
Comet Catcher	Ancient World
Drones	Tuskegee Airmen
Fault Lines	Virtual Reality
Gnarly Sports Injuries	Wild Weather
Great Spies of the World	Witchcraft
Hacked	Wormholes
Little Rock Nine	

Photo credits: Cover: Everett Collection Historical / Alamy Stock Photo; page iv/1: Nagel Photography / Shutterstock.com; page 6: Everett Historical / Shutterstock.com; page 7: Everett Historical / Shutterstock.com; page 9: Bettmann / Getty Images; page 12: mark reinstein / Alamy Stock Photo; page 13: Carl Iwasaki / Getty Images; page14: Carl Iwasaki / Getty Images; pages 16/17: stock_photo_world / Shutterstock.com; page 16: Keystone Pictures USA / Alamy Stock Photo; page 18: Everett Collection Inc / Alamy Stock Photo; page 26: Don Cravens / Getty Images; pages 28/29: Francis Miller / Getty Images; pages 30/31: Everett Collection Inc / Alamy Stock Photo; page 31: MPI / Stringer/ Getty Images; page 32: Everett Collection Inc / Alamy Stock Photo; page 33: Popperfoto / Getty Images; page 34: World History Archive / Alamy Stock Photo; page 35: RBM Vintage Images / Alamy Stock Photo; page 35: Alpha Historica / Alamy Stock Photo; page 37: Bettmann / Getty Images; page 38: Everett Collection Inc / Alamy Stock Photo; page 39: nsf / Alamy Stock Photo; page 40: John Bryson / Getty Images; page 41: John Bryson / Getty Images; pages 42/43: Everett Collection Historical / Alamy Stock Photo; page 43: John Bryson / Getty Images; page 44: Bettmann/ Getty Images; page 45: Everett Collection Historical / Alamy Stock Photo; page 46: Everett Collection Inc / Alamy Stock Photo; page 47: Bill Eppridge / Getty Images; page 48: JOYCE NALTCHAYAN / Getty Images; page 49: Bettmann / Contributor; All other source images from Shutterstock.com

SADDLEBACK
EDUCATIONAL PUBLISHING
www.sdlback.com

ISBN-13: 978-1-68021-055-2
ISBN-10: 1-68021-055-6
eBook: 978-1-63078-382-2

Printed in Malaysia

22 21 20 19 18   1 2 3 4 5

TABLE OF CONTENTS

Chapter 1
A LONG JOURNEY

It was the 1950s.
Linda Brown was 7 years old.
She lived in Topeka, Kansas.

Linda was in third grade.
Her school was far away.
She walked six blocks.
Then she rode a bus.
Finally she got to school.
It was a long trip.

4

There was a school that was closer.

It was near Linda's house.

Linda wanted to go there.

But she was not allowed.

That school was for white children.

Linda was African American.

She was not welcome.

Chapter 2
THE WAY THINGS WERE

Life was different back then.

Many states had special *laws*.

They kept blacks and whites apart.

These were called *Jim Crow laws*.

These laws were not fair.
Rules were based on color.
Blacks had to sit in the back of buses.
They could not eat with whites.
Whites and blacks could not marry.

WAITING ROOM
FOR COLORED ONLY
BY ORDER
POLICE DEPT.

Words of History
Freedom Rider: a person
who tested laws saying that
people could not be treated
differently while traveling
using buses and trains in
the South

Some wanted change.
They wanted people to be treated
the same.
Their goal was *equality*.

WE MARCH FOR
INTEGRATED SCHOOLS NOW!

Back then, schools were based on color too.
"Separate but equal" was the law.
Segregation was allowed.
But the schools had to be equal.

It did not work out that way.
The schools were separate.
But they were not equal.

White schools had new books.

There were many teachers.

Black schools were different.

Roofs leaked.

Students read old books.

There were few teachers.

Some towns had little money.

So they built only one school.

White children went there.

Black children had to go to another town.

They would travel to a black school.

Chapter 3
BUILDING A CASE

Linda Brown was in third grade.

She could not go to the white school.

The black school was far away.

It took a long time to get there.

Her father was mad.

This was not okay.

He wanted her at a school close by.

He tried to *enroll* Linda in a white school.

Linda would get a better education there.

Other black parents did the same thing.

The school said no.

The families went to *court*.

"Separate but equal" is wrong, they said.

They wanted the law changed.

The *case* was big.

It went to the *Supreme Court*.

This is the top court in the US.

It decides cases for the country.

Words of History

The case was called *Brown v. Board of Education.*

The Supreme Court has nine *judges*.
They hear both sides of a story.
Their decisions are final.

Changes can happen because of
what is decided.
People may disagree.
But they have to obey.
They must do what the court says.

Chapter 4
THE COURT DECIDES

It was 1954.

Earl Warren was the Chief Justice.

That is the top judge on the Supreme Court.

Warren did not like segregation.

He wanted to change the law.

It was unfair to black children, he thought.

The way they were treated was wrong.

He thought schools were for all.

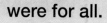

The other judges agreed.

They felt the same way.

The case was done.

It was the end of "separate but equal."

The law had changed.

Black children could now go to white schools.

But not everyone was ready.

Words of History

Thurgood Marshall: An African American lawyer who helped the Little Rock Nine. He later became the first African American Supreme Court judge.

Chapter 5
LITTLE ROCK

Linda Brown was happy.

So was her father.

But the case had taken a while.

She had gotten older.

By then, she was in junior high.

Linda went to an integrated school.

It was near her home.

Many liked the new law.

Black children could go to white schools.

Their families were happy.

Others were mad.

They lived in the South.

This was their way of life.

They did not want to change.

Some fought the *ruling*.

Integration was the law in the US.

But things did not go smoothly.

It was bad in some places.

One of those places was Little

Rock, Arkansas.

Little Rock had a plan.

The school board decided.

They would follow the law.

But it would happen slowly.

Integration would start in 1957.

The high schools would be first.

They asked for *volunteers*.

Black students could go to a white school.

The school was Central High School.

But it was not that simple.

They would not be able to play sports.

Band was off limits too.

So was choir.

People were upset.

They did not like the plan.

Some black parents were warned.

Their bosses would fire them.

Many students chose to stay.

They stayed at the black schools.

It was safer.

Black leaders helped.

They convinced some students to go.

Central High was a nice school.

They would be the first blacks to attend.

LITTLE ROCK CENTRAL HIGH SCHOOL

Chapter 6
THE GOVERNOR DISAGREES

Orval Faubus was the governor of Arkansas.

He did not like the plan.

So he made a plan of his own.

He said the US government was wrong.

It was forcing a state to change.

People did not want this.

It was against the people's will, he said.

He said there would be violence.

Blacks needed to stay at their own schools.

This was for safety, he said.

27

Faubus called in the *National Guard*.

This is a group of soldiers.

They report to the governor.

He is in charge.

The Guard went to Central High.

They had a job.

Keep blacks out.

Chapter 7
THE BIG DAY

It was September 4, 1957.

This was the first day of school.

Things were tense at Central High.

Soldiers stood outside.

A mob did too.

They were angry.

People shouted.

They waved signs.

Black students were not welcome.

Elizabeth Eckford was 15.
She was one of the black students.
Today was to be her first day at a
white school.
She had made a dress.
It was a special day.

The Little Rock Nine

She got to the school.

It was time to go inside.

The crowd was angry.

They shouted at her.

Some called her bad names.

Others spit on her.

Elizabeth was scared.

Her knees shook.

"Go home!" someone yelled.

Others chanted.

"Two! Four! Six! Eight!

We ain't gonna integrate!"

Elizabeth tried to enter the school.

She did not get far.

Soldiers stopped her.

She went home.

Other black students did too.

Chapter 8
THE PRESIDENT STEPS IN

A fight had begun.

Some wanted to stop Faubus.

Others agreed with him.

They went to court.

A judge decided.

He said the governor was wrong.

Legal battles went on.

Martin Luther King Jr. got involved.

He was a *civil rights* leader.

King called Dwight D. Eisenhower.

That was the president.

King wanted him to step in.

The president was in Newport, Rhode Island.

He was on vacation.

But he saw everything on TV.

It made him angry.

He supported the Supreme Court.

But he was worried about Little Rock.

Things were tense.

People were mad.

They were ready to fight.

He thought things could get violent.

He had to talk to Faubus.

Faubus went to Newport.
The two men spoke.
They tried to work things out.
Faubus said he would back off.
Black students could go to Central High.
The Guard would protect them.

But Faubus lied to the president.

He told the Guard to leave.

The students tried to enter the school again.

A *riot* started.

Faubus did nothing to stop it.

Eisenhower was furious.

It was time to call in the Army.

The troops went to Little Rock.

They would help the black students.

There was another order.
He took over the Guard.
Faubus was no longer in charge.
Eisenhower was.

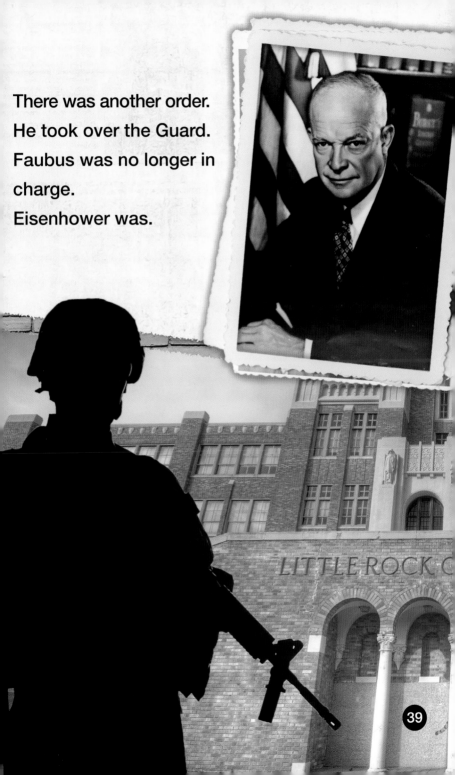

LITTLE ROCK C

Chapter 9
TROOPS ARRIVE

It was September 24, 1957.
Troops arrived.
There were more than a thousand.
Some called it an *invasion*.

Eisenhower was not happy.
But he felt he had to act.

Words of History

President Eisenhower sent in the 101st Airborne, an elite division of the United States Army. They were known as the "Screaming Eagles."

It was the next day.
Soldiers stood guard.
They held rifles.
There were *bayonets* on top.

Nine black students were there.
They entered the school.
Soldiers kept them safe.

On the magazine cover:

LIFE

BEGINNING, A STUNNING 'LIFE' SERIES
MAN'S NEW WORLD
PART 1: TECHNICAL TRIUMPHS TO SHAPE DAILY LIVES

LITTLE ROCK CENTRAL

U.S. TROOPS
TAKE OVER
IN ARKANSAS

OCTOBER 7, 1957   **25** CENTS

They got inside.

But they did not feel welcome.

Things were still very tense.

Change would take time.

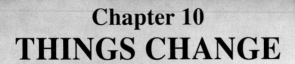

Chapter 10
THINGS CHANGE

The Little Rock Nine stayed.

They went to school every day.

But it was not easy.

People were not kind.

The teens stood tall.

Eight finished the year.

THIS SCHOOL **CLOSED** *BY ORDER OF THE* *EDERAL GOVERMENT*

The next school year came.

But the governor had made a decision.

He closed all the high schools.

Blacks could not attend.

Whites could not either.

There was no school all year.

Some call it "the lost year."

45

It was August 1959.

Schools reopened.

White students came back.

So did black students.

They were still not welcome.

Mobs stood outside.

People inside were cruel.

But they did not give up.

Other schools started to integrate.
It was a hard process.
Sometimes it took years.

Fifty years went by.

It was 2007.

The Little Rock Nine came back.

Central High was fully integrated.

Current students heard the story.

It started with pain.

There was *racism*, hatred, and *prejudice*.

But things changed.

These nine people helped.

Their bravery made a difference.

GLOSSARY

bayonet: a knife attached to the end of a rifle

case: a matter that will be decided in court

civil rights: basic rights that the government applies to all people

court: a place where legal cases are heard

enroll: to sign up to participate in something

equality: having the same rights as others

integration: a policy that brings people of different races, genders, and religions together

invasion: the act of going to a place to take it over

Jim Crow laws: rules that kept blacks and whites apart

judge: a person who has the authority to make decisions on legal cases

law: the system of rules made by the government

National Guard: a military group that is assigned to support a state

prejudice: a feeling of dislike for someone that is based on their race, gender, or religion

racism: poor treatment of people based on the color of their skin or their background

riot: a violent event when a number of people are out of control and dangerous

ruling: an official decision made by a judge

segregation: the practice of keeping people apart from each other because of race, religion, or gender

separate but equal: a legal policy that said people of different races had to live, work, and go to school in different places but that those places should be of the same quality

Supreme Court: the highest court in the US

volunteer: someone who offers to do something without being paid or forced

TUSKEGEE AIRMEN

Chapter 1
RED TAILS

1944.
World War II.
Up in the sky.
U.S. planes.
All are *bombers*.
They have a job.
To blow up an oil field.
It will hurt the enemy.
Slow down the war.

The planes are big.
And loud.
They are slow.
Easy targets.

One man would not give up.
Yancey Williams.
He was black.
And a pilot.
He had a goal.
To join the U.S. Army Air Corps.
He passed the tests.
The Army still said no.
He went to court.
Fought for his *rights*.
It worked.

Chapter 5

THE EXPERIMENT

The Army changed its rules.
It did not want a court fight.
So it made a new unit.
The 99th Pursuit *Squadron*.
A group of planes.
Flown by blacks.
Williams saw this as a win.
He joined the unit.

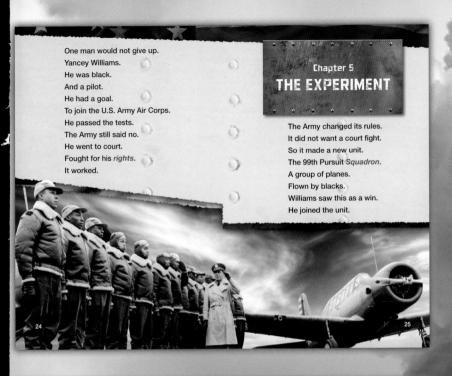

March 7, 1942.
A big day at Tuskegee.
The first class earned its wings.
Five men.
All ready to fly.

Who would lead them?
Benjamin O. Davis Jr.
He went to the U.S. Military Academy.
All the other *cadets* were white.
They did not talk to him.
But he stayed.
Studied hard.
And *graduated*.

Davis became an officer.
The Army chose him.
He would lead the 99th.
He had one goal.
"To lead this squadron to victory."

red rhino books®

NONFICTION

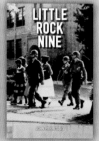

9781680210736 9781680210316 9781680210729 9781680210484

9781680210347 9781680210477 9781680210293 9781680210538

9781680210712 9781680210491 9781680210378 9781680210552

WWW.REDRHINOBOOKS.COM

9781680210545   9781680210286   9781680210309   9781680210507

9781680210354   9781680210521   9781680210361   9781680210514

9781680210323   9781680210330

MORE
TITLES
COMING
SOON